Specials!

Punctuation

Mary Green

Acknowledgements

p62 'whatspunctuation' © John Foster 2004 from *Our Teacher's Gone Bananas* (Oxford University Press)

United Kingdom: Folens Publishers, Apex Business Centre, Boscombe Road, Dunstable, LU5 4RL.

Email: folens@folens.com

Ireland: Folens Publishers, Greenhills Road, Tallaght, Dublin 24.

Email: info@folens.ie

Poland: JUKA, ul. Renesansowa 38, Warsaw 01-905.

Editor: Jennifer Steele   Layout artist: Book Matrix, India   Illustrations: Lee Sullivan
Cover design: Holbrook Design   Cover image: Corbis

First published 2006 by Folens Limited.

British Library Cataloguing in Publication Data. A catalogue record for this publication is available from the British Library.

ISBN 1 84303 867 6 / 978 1 84303 867 2

Contents

Introduction

Specials! *English Punctuation* is divided into ten units that include a series of photocopiable Activity sheets and sometimes Resource sheets. Each unit focuses on an aspect of punctuation and links to the English Framework. The first unit looks at the difference between speech and writing, encouraging students to recognise that punctuation helps us to make sense of what we read. This in turn gives them a better understanding of the need for punctuation in their own writing.

The teacher can work in different ways. For example, a unit could be taught as a lesson with students in groups of varying sizes. Alternatively, a single Activity sheet or Resource sheet could be used as support material.

The Teacher's notes give guidance and are laid out as follows:

Objectives

These are the main skills or knowledge to be learned.

Prior knowledge

This refers to the minimum skills or knowledge required by students to complete the tasks. As a rule, students should have a reading comprehension age of six to nine years and should be working at levels 1 to 3. Some student pages are more challenging than others and you will need to select accordingly.

English Framework links

All units link to aspects of the English Framework at Key Stage 3 and details are given.

Scottish attainment targets

Links are given to the Scottish 5–14 National Guidelines.

Background

This gives additional information related to punctuation.

Starter activity

Since the units can be taught as a lesson, a warm-up activity focusing on an aspect of the unit is suggested.

Resource sheets and Activity sheets

The Resource sheet contains no tasks and can be used as a stimulus for discussion. Related tasks are provided on the Activity sheets.

Plenary

The teacher can use the suggestions here to do additional work, recap on the main points covered, reinforce a particular idea or ask students to carry out assessments.

Assessment sheet

At the end of the book is an Assessment sheet focusing on student progress. It can be used in different ways. A student could complete it as self-assessment, while his or her teacher also completes one on the student's progress. They can then compare the two. This is useful in situations where the teacher or classroom assistant is working with one student. Alternatively, students could work in partners to carry out peer assessments and then compare the outcomes with each other.

Starting from a simple base that students can manage, the Assessment sheet allows the student to discuss his or her own progress, consider different points of view, discuss how he or she might improve and allow the teacher to see the work from the student's perspective. A completed sample assessment is given here.

Assessment sheet

Tick the boxes to show what you know or what you can do

	Know/ Yes	Not sure/ Sometimes	Don't know/ No
1. I listen to the teacher.	✓		
2. I can work well with a partner.		✓	
3. I can work well in a group.			✓
4. I know what a full stop is and where it comes in a sentence.	✓		
5. I know the difference between a full stop and a comma.		✓	
6. I can use commas to separate words in a list.	✓		
7. I can use commas to separate parts of a sentence.			✓

I know best / I can do best: ....

I need to: (Write no more than three targets)
....
....
....

Teacher's notes

Speech and writing

Objectives

- Understand that there is a difference between speech and writing
- Understand what a sentence is and the need for punctuation
- Distinguish between sentences and non-sentences

Prior knowledge

Students need to have experience of writing in sentences, although these may not always be accurate. They need to be able to write words and phrases and have an awareness of how full stops are used. Their handwriting should be legible.

English Framework links

Yr7 Sentence level 3; Yr8 Sentence level 3; Yr9 Sentence level 2

Scottish attainment targets

English Language – Listening
Strand – Listening in order to respond to texts
Level C
English Language – Writing
Strand – Punctuation and structure
Level C

Background

A student who does not write (or writes intermittently) in sentences may lack sufficient writing experience or have specific learning difficulties. One student may sense a difference between speech and writing, but not be able to use the conventions of writing. Another student may write in Non-standard English and use Non-standard grammar, but be writing in sentences – at the least using full stops and probably other punctuation. Either way, it is useful for students to look at some of the differences between speech and writing. This unit focuses on what a sentence is and why we write in sentences. Different Activity sheets can be used with students of different abilities.

Starter activity

Read the Resource sheet, 'What Happened yesterday?', to students. It records, in writing, speech as it is spoken, so there is little punctuation beyond ellipses. Read it with expression so that students grasp the change in voice (for example, in the first line the repetition, 'yeah … Sunday' would be written 'Yeah! Sunday …'). Also use gesture. Do not refer to the annotations yet. Simply ask students to comment on how the reading was communicated. (You may also wish to discuss the content and dangers involved.)

Resource sheets and Activity sheets

Give out the Resource sheet, 'What happened yesterday?', to students and discuss the annotations. Ask them how it differs from writing in sentences. Students should then work with partners to talk about something funny or unusual that has happened to them, or what they did the day before, observing how each other communicates. They can record their comments on the Activity sheet, 'Communication'. Point to any features they have missed and discuss how we communicate in a range of ways that are not available to us in writing.

'What happened yesterday?' has been rewritten in sentences on the second Resource sheet, 'From speech to sentences'. Compare the two with students who write in sentences but have difficulty writing in Standard English. For those who are not writing in sentences, you or a learning support assistant can read the first few lines aloud and ask students to identify where the full stops come.

The remaining Resource sheet, 'What is a sentence?' and the Activity sheet, 'Sentences or not?', can also be used with those students who are not writing in sentences. (Some may be able to distinguish between sentences and non-sentences, but still not write coherently.) An adult should work with the students to go through 'What is a sentence?'. Students can then complete 'Sentences or not?' on their own, or with help, depending on progress.

Plenary

Recap on the difference between speech and writing and the other main points taught. If students have completed 'Sentences or not?' on their own, discuss their answers with them.

What happened yesterday?

☞ Keep this to compare with the Resource sheet, 'From speech to sentences'.

hesitation (pause)   change of tenses

yesterday ... let's see ... it was Sunday ... yeah ... Sunday ... that boy fell in the lake ... he was messin' about ... y'know ... being stupid like ... and we saw it ... that's Lena and me ... we met up ... Lena and me...and we went up the park ... no ... uh ... we goes to the shop first ... the shop on the corner ... the corner of my road ... to get some chocolate ... um ... then we goes up the park ... well just to hang out really ... it was a sunny day ... and there's these boys ... older boys.... used to go to our school ... well they're chucking stuff in the lake ... the lake by the Wood Lane entrance ... y'know where I mean ... at the back ... the big lake...well you should a seen it ... this boy he's pushin' this other boy ... not fightin' like ... just being stupid ... and then ... he slips ... this boy he slips ... just like that ... whoosh he's in the lake ... and it's deep there y'know ... and these other boys they're just laughin' ... and this boy he's ... he's splashin' about ... and they're just laughin' ... but then they stop ... 'cos this boy ... he can't swim ... so they have to pull him out ... and he's so mad ... he is SO mad ... it was a right laugh

repetition (repeated words)   slang

English Punctuation

Activity sheet – Speech and writing

Communication

Ask a partner to tell you something funny or unusual that has happened to him or her, or what he or she did yesterday. Listen carefully. Think about whether he or she:

- paused
- said the same things more than once
- used body language (for example, use of hands)
- changed his or her voice
- used slang.

☞ Make notes in the boxes. Give examples.

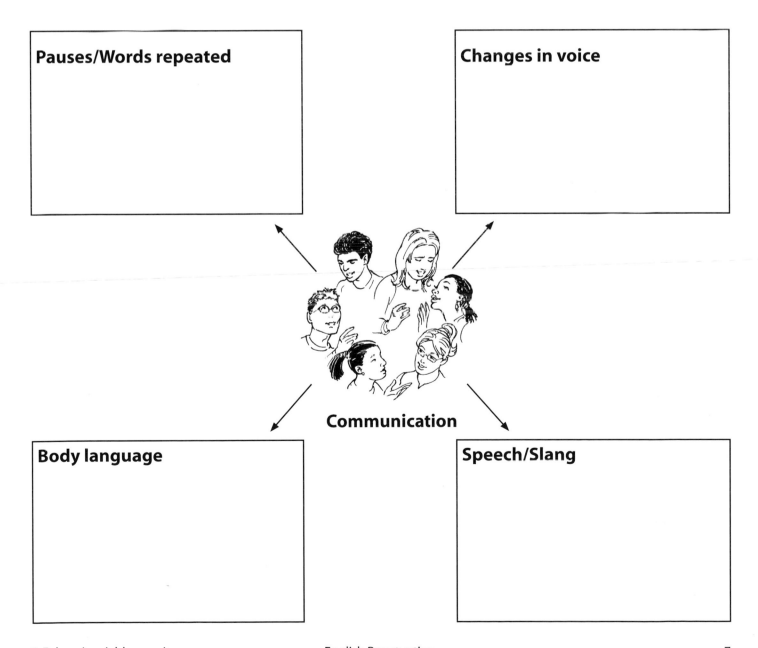

Pauses/Words repeated

Changes in voice

Communication

Body language

Speech/Slang

Resource sheet – Speech and writing

From speech to sentences

☞ Compare this with the Resource sheet, 'What happened yesterday?'
The labels show what has changed. What else has changed?

Capital letters, full stops replace ellipses.

Standard English replaces 'Lena and me'.

It was Sunday yesterday, the day the boy fell into the lake. It all happened because he was being silly. My friend, Lena and I saw it all.

After we had been to the shop to buy some chocolate, we went to the park. It was a sunny day and we like to wander about there. Some older boys – boys that used to go to our school – were throwing rubbish into the lake at the Wood Lane entrance. They were pushing each other and playing around. Then one of them slipped, and suddenly, whoosh! He was in the water, just like that! It's deep at that part of the lake but the others carried on laughing while he was splashing and spluttering. Finally, they realised he couldn't swim. So they had to haul him out. He didn't like it. He didn't like it at all. He was really angry, but it was all a good laugh really.

Exclamation mark to stress words.

Sentences are of different lengths.

English Punctuation
© Folens (copiable page)

What is a sentence?

A sentence is a group of words that makes sense on its own and feels complete.
It allows the reader to understand what he or she is reading.

A sentence begins with a capital letter.

It ends with a full stop.

He goes to school on his old bike.

It can also end with a question mark or an exclamation mark.

Does he go to school on his old bike?
He goes to school on his old bike!

A sentence can also be of different lengths.

He rode his old bike.
He rode his old bike up the path, straight through the gate and along the road.

A sentence can start in different ways.

After he rode his old bike up the path, he rode straight through the gate.
His sister was watching to see if he would fall off his old bike.

Sentences or not?

A sentence is a group of words that makes sense on its own and feels complete. It allows the reader to understand what he or she is reading.

☞ Which are sentences? Put a tick by them.
Then turn the others into sentences. Write them underneath.

Last week we went to see a film. ☐

The whole family went. ☐

Gran loved the film because ☐

My older brother ☐

My dad fell asleep and began to snore. ☐

So, my Mum ☐

My younger sister cried. ☐

It was one of the ☐

After the film we ☐

About 10:00pm ☐

English Punctuation

Teacher's notes

Capital letters/full stops

Objectives

- Use full stops and capital letters
- Use capital letters accurately in a variety of ways
- Write in sentences and short paragraphs
- Carry out proofreading using symbols
- Understand that the formality of English changes in context

Prior knowledge

Students should be increasingly writing in sentences, using full stops and capital letters. Their handwriting should be legible.

English Framework links

Yr7 Sentence level 3, Writing 1; Yr8 Sentence level 3, Writing 1; Yr9 Sentence level 2

Scottish attainment targets

English Language – Writing
Strand – Punctuation and structure
Level C
Strand – Functional writing
Level D

Background

This follows on from the previous unit, 'Speech and writing'. Students have to construct sentences accurately. Capitalisation in other contexts, as well as in sentences, is also included. The use of capitals for the pronoun 'I', for the names of people and places, days of the week, months and in titles is covered. These will need reinforcing regularly. Students are also taught proofreading and the layout of a letter.

Starter activity

If students have completed the first unit, 'Speech and writing', recap on the features of sentences or ask students to explain the function of the capital letter and full stop (that is, to mark boundaries and help the reader to make sense of what has been written).

In pairs, ask students to think of three examples of where we use capitals (for example, their own names). Discuss proofreading with them and go through the proofreading symbols provided in the unit.

Activity sheets

The first three Activity sheets are suitable for those students who are still learning to write in sentences and to use capitals. In the first sheet, 'Beginnings and endings', students are reminded what a sentence is and how it is punctuated. In the second sheet, 'Names and places', they are introduced to the use of capitals in other contexts. (See Background for details.) There are similar tasks in the third sheet, 'My favourite things'. Here they are also asked to write three sentences using a frame.

The Activity sheet, 'The letter', is a harder task and students need to be able to recognise sentence boundaries, capitals for names and dates to complete it satisfactorily. (You could ask those students who experience difficulty to attempt the passage and note the extent to which they can correct it.)

In the final Activity sheet, 'An email to William', students are asked to convert an email into a formal letter. A model is provided of the latter, enabling students to focus on the punctuation (which needs correction) and also layout. This task is suitable for students who have grasped capitalisation and basic punctuation. Point to the use of the pronoun 'I' as a capital.

Plenary

Recap on the uses of the capital letter. Students should think of as many examples as possible of where it is used. Ask them if they can remember when it isn't used (for example, minor words in titles).

Beginnings and endings

> **Remember**
> A sentence begins with a capital letter.
> It ends with a full stop.

1. Read these sentence beginnings.
2. Choose endings from the box below and complete the sentences.
3. Punctuate them correctly. Use a red pen and these proofreading symbols.

⊙ full stop   Ξ capital letters

Beginnings

_____

a small envelope

_____

rob's mother

_____

when she

_____

a dark frown

_____

the family dog

_____

Endings

saw it lying on the mat

spread over her face and she bit her lip

dropped through the letter box

barked and seemed to know what was in the letter

picked it up she saw it came from Rob's school

English Punctuation

Activity sheet – Capital letters/full stops

Names and places

The names of people and places start with capital letters.

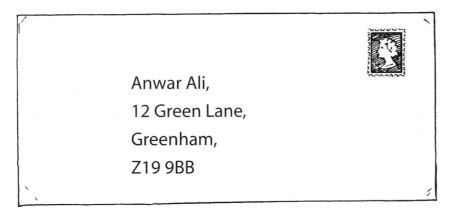

Anwar Ali,
12 Green Lane,
Greenham,
Z19 9BB

1. Write the address of your school correctly on the envelope below.

2. Put capital letters in the correct places below. Write the answers at the side.

jackie bond _____   high street _____

bull lane _____   france _____

london _____   snowdon _____

north sea _____   mr j goody _____

leroy smith _____   dr kumar _____

edinburgh _____   rome _____

My favourite things

Titles have capital letters in them. For example:

It Came from Outer Space

The beginning word and the main words have capital letters. Small words do not have capitals.

1. Make a list of your favourite things under these headings. Remember to use capital letters in the right places.

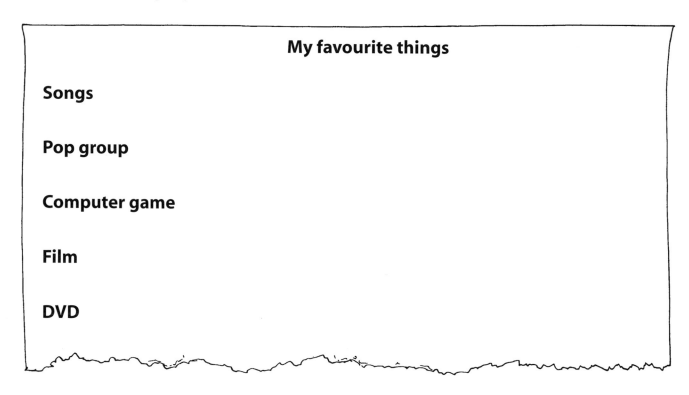

My favourite things

Songs

Pop group

Computer game

Film

DVD

2. Choose one thing and write three sentences about why it is your favourite.

I have chosen _____ because _____

It is also _____

In addition, _____

English Punctuation

Activity sheet – Capital letters/full stops

The letter

1. Correct the paragraph using proofreading signs:

⊙ full stop   ☰ capital letters

> rob's mother read the letter it was from rob's school
>
> it was dated monday 25th june she didn't like what she read it
>
> seemed rob hadn't been to school for a week and his class teacher
>
> mr bell wanted to know why it was not the first time rob had stayed
>
> away and rob's mum knew it would not be the last she was angry in
>
> the morning she would have to go up to the school to see the
>
> headteacher mrs beech that was not something to look forward to
>
> suddenly the front door banged it was rob

2. What happened next? Write a paragraph below using the writing frame.

> He opened the door _____
>
> _____
>
> His mother _____
>
> _____
>
> In her hand _____
>
> _____
>
> Rob knew _____
>
> _____

An email to William

☞ Read this email from Philip Henslowe to William Shakespeare.

From: philip.henslowe@rose.com
Subject: play
Date: 8 July 13:25:05
To: william.shakespeare@hamlet.com

Hi Will
Can u update me on the play? R u ready to send script? Deadline last week.

We r waiting
Henslowe

philip.henslowe@rose.com

Rose Alley
Bankside
London
SW1

☞ Write the email as a more formal letter. Use the model below, *but change the mistakes first*. Remember to use capital letters.

mr wlliam shakespeare,
the boar inn,
fish street,
london

Date

dear

as you must be aware …

i would be grateful …

yours truly,

Philip Henslowe's address

English Punctuation

Teacher's notes

Question marks/exclamation marks

Objectives

- Use question marks when writing a question
- Use exclamation marks appropriately to add emphasis
- Carry out proofreading using symbols

Prior knowledge

Students should be able to recognise sentences, read simple texts with expression and be writing in sentences, using full stops and capital letters. Their handwriting should be legible.

English Framework links

Yr7 Sentence level 3, Writing 1; Yr8 Sentence level 3, Writing 1; Yr9 Sentence level 2

Scottish attainment targets

English Language – Writing
Strand – Punctuation and structure
Level C
Strand – Knowledge about language
Level C

Background

Since students should now be using capital letters and full stops in their writing, it is useful to remind them what punctuation helps us to do. In speech we hesitate and pause erratically, and while written punctuation is not used in quite the same way it nonetheless helps us to convey meaning by imposing order on written language. Encouraging early readers to change intonation as they read helps them to understand the need for punctuation. In this regard, the question mark and exclamation mark can promote reading with expression.

Starter activity

Introduce the question mark. Then ask students questions and tell them to ask each other questions. Point to the change in intonation.

Activity sheets

The first Activity sheet, 'Question marks', explains the difference between a question and a statement. Students are asked to distinguish between the two. Students are also given 'wh' question words and other question structures to help them to write their own questions.

In the Activity sheet, 'Corny jokes', note that as well as question marks and capital letters at the beginning of sentences, 'Dracula's' should also have a capital letter and in the last joke an exclamation mark would be used in 'Don't be silly!' Ask students which part of each joke is written in sentences and which part isn't (with the exception of 7 and 8).

For the Activity sheet, 'Question setting', students should work out the answers on their own, then read the whole conversation with a partner, taking it in turns to read a part each. Remind students to add question marks to the questions. Also illustrate how to read a question with expression, contrasting it with a statement.

Exclamation marks are often overused and students are encouraged to discriminate carefully when they complete the Activity sheets, 'Exclamation marks' and 'Headlines'. In the former, questions 3, 5 and 6 should not have exclamation marks; in the latter 3, 4 and 7 should and 1 and 6 should have question marks.

Plenary

Ask students how they can tell if someone is asking a question from the sound of their voice. Then ask them how they know what a question is in writing. They should note the use of 'wh' words as well as the use of question marks. Also recap on the use of the exclamation mark.

Question marks

● A statement is different from a question and has different punctuation.

We have to go there again. ◄─────────── full stop

● When we want to ask a question in writing we use a question mark.

Why do we have to go to there again? ◄────── question mark

☞ Decide which sentences are questions and which are statements.
Add a full stop or a question mark.

1. I bought a new mobile phone yesterday
2. When I switched it on nothing happened
3. Would you believe it
4. I tried again, but it wouldn't work
5. It's not good enough
6. Can you guess how much it cost me

☞ Many words help us to write questions. Finish these questions. Remember to add
question marks.

1. Why did _____

2. When can _____

3. Where is _____

4. What kind of _____

5. Who was _____

6. Are you _____

7. Can they _____

8. Will she _____

Corny jokes

Read these jokes. Then punctuate them so that they make sense, using capital letters, full stops, question marks and exclamation marks.

Use these proofreading signs and a red pen to correct them.

⊙ full stop   ☰ capital letters   *p* other punctuation

1. what's green and makes you itch spinach

2. what vegetable has a nasty bite a turnip

3. how do you make upside-down pudding by standing on your head

4. what's a runner's favourite food hurry and rice and tomato catchup

5. what do you get if you cross a baker with a firework bunpowder

6. what's dracula's favourite food a bloody stake

7. how many elephants does it take to eat a hundred sausage sandwiches none elephants don't like sausage sandwiches

8. how many popstars does it take to make a hotdog don't be silly you don't have pop stars in hotdogs

Question setting

Two teenagers are talking on the phone. Here is one side of the conversation. Read what Jack says. Then work out what the questions are from the answers he gives. Write them down. The first has been done for you.

Hullo, who is it?

It's me, Jack.

_____

I'm fine.

_____

Yeah, I'm going to the match with my sister.

_____

We could meet up first if you like.

_____

By the clock tower or the park gates.

_____

Yeah, the clock tower is the best place.

_____

About 1 o'clock.

_____

2 o'clock is fine.

_____

Yeah, my sister can make 2 o'clock as well. OK – see you then. Bye.

Exclamation marks

We use an exclamation mark to express feeling. It tells the reader that the words are stressed.

Look at that pass<u>!</u>   *It's a goal<u>!</u>*

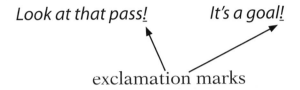

exclamation marks

☞ Decide which sentences need exclamation marks and add them. Put full stops by the rest.

1. Let's go now

2. That's fantastic, I can hardly believe it

3. I know this is hard, but you must wait quietly

4. Watch out, you're going to drop that egg

5. That's a truly excellent piece of work

6. I love to play cricket In the summer

7. Oh no, he's lost his bag for the third time

8. Ready, steady go

9. Instead of lazing in the chair all day, do something

● Compare your answers with a partner.

Headlines

☞ Decide whether these headlines need:

- exclamation marks
- question marks
- capital letters.

Use proofreading signs and red pen to correct them.

≡ capital letters   *p* exclamation marks/question marks

> **Remember**
> Headlines do not have full stops.

1. smith versus james but who'll win

2. my family nightmare

3. **not over my dead body**

4. man u are back

5. chaos as traffic piles up

6. **are FA rules set to change**

7. vanished

8. **rough ride in winter weather**

9. top tv star in pub brawl

10. lottery winner gives half to charity

Teacher's notes

Commas

Objectives

- Distinguish between commas and full stops
- Use commas to separate words in a list and in sentences
- Use commas at the boundaries between main clauses and sub-clauses
- Learn that the absence of a comma can alter meaning

Prior knowledge

Students should recognise sentences, be reading simple texts with expression and be writing in sentences using full stops, capital letters, question marks and exclamation marks. Their handwriting should be legible.

English Framework links

Yr7 Sentence level 1, 3, Writing 1; Yr8 Sentence level 1, 3; Writing 1, Yr9 Sentence level 2

Scottish attainment targets

English Language – Writing
Strand – Punctuation and structure
Level C
Strand – Knowledge about language
Level C

Background

There is some debate about how often we should use commas and increasingly fewer commas are used in sentences. For example, nowadays they are less frequently used to separate phrases, but a hundred years ago or more they were common, as were semi-colons, because sentences tended to be longer. A glance at any of Dickens' novels will confirm this. The comma is nonetheless essential in certain situations and without it meaning can become ambiguous or changed. To make the point, a poem that is also a riddle is included in the unit. See the Resource sheet, 'I have a pig with yellow wings'. It is based on the seventeenth-century poem, 'I saw a peacock with a fiery tail' (Anon.), which was printed in 1671 in *Westminster Drollery, Or a Choice Collection of the Newest Songs and Poems both at Court and Theaters*.

Starter activity

Use the Starter activity to introduce the comma and compare its function to that of the full stop. Point out to students that a sentence should never end with a comma. This is reinforced throughout the unit.

Resource sheets and Activity sheets

The first Activity sheet, 'List them', focuses on commas used in lists. Most students should be able to do this without difficulty.

The next three sheets look at commas in sentences and also main clauses and subordinate clauses. Use the first of these, the Resource sheet, 'Commas in sentences', to explain how commas function. Students can keep it for reference. The next Activity sheet, 'Clauses', introduces the terms 'main clause' and 'sub-clause'. The third Activity sheet, 'Commas and clauses', is more challenging. Students are given exercises to complete. All of these require commas, so sub-clauses beginning 'that …' are not included, since no commas would be required. For example: *The diving board, which was very high, was at the far end of the swimming baths./The diving board that was very high was at the far end of the swimming baths.* Providing students have grasped the earlier points they could work on their own, though you may prefer to teach these three sheets together to the whole group.

Conclude with the Resource sheet, 'I have a pig with yellow wings', which illustrates the importance of the comma. Use it to contrast the nonsense meaning with the logical. For example:

I have a pig.
With yellow wings I have a butterfly,
Growing on my lawn I have a weed,
Of tartan cloth I have a cloak,

and so on.

Plenary

Recap on the uses of the comma: to separate words in lists and in sentences.

List them

We use commas to separate items in a list. For example:

nails, hammer, drill

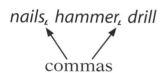

commas

1. Yasmin has made a list of jobs she has to do on her computer. She has left out the commas. Put them in.

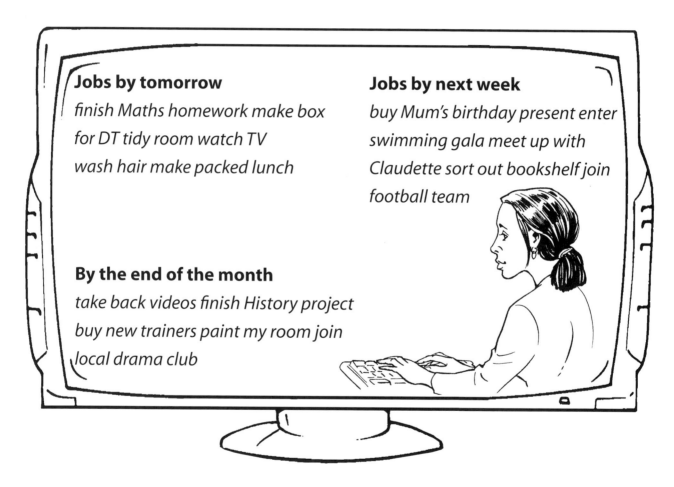

Jobs by tomorrow
finish Maths homework make box for DT tidy room watch TV wash hair make packed lunch

Jobs by next week
buy Mum's birthday present enter swimming gala meet up with Claudette sort out bookshelf join football team

By the end of the month
take back videos finish History project buy new trainers paint my room join local drama club

2. Make a list of jobs you have to do for tomorrow and by next week.

Jobs by tomorrow	Jobs by next week

English Punctuation

Commas in sentences

Commas can separate different parts of a sentence. Here are three examples.

1. This is the main part of the sentence.

Denzil and his friend, Ajay, lived in the same street.

Two commas separate the extra information, 'Ajay'.

● 'Denzil and his friend lived in the same street.' makes sense without 'Ajay'.

2. This is the main part of the sentence.

Jackson, who was Denzil's younger brother, sometimes went swimming with Denzil and Ajay.

Two commas separate the extra information, 'who was Denzil's younger brother'.

● 'Jackson sometimes went swimming with Denzil and Ajay.' makes sense without 'who was Denzil's younger brother'.

3. This is the main part of the sentence.

Calling out to him, Ajay ran towards Denzil.

One comma separates the extra information, 'Calling out to him'.

● 'Ajay ran towards Denzil.' makes sense without 'Calling out to him'.

Clauses

The main part of a sentence is called a **clause**. *It makes sense on its own.* The extra part is called the **sub-clause.** *It does not make sense on its own.*

Look at this example again.

Main part of the sentence or main clause.

Jackson, who was Denzil's younger brother, sometimes went swimming with Denzil and Ajay.

Extra information or sub-clause.

- 'Jackson sometimes went swimming with Denzil and Ajay.' Makes sense without 'who was Denzil's younger brother'.

☞ Underline the main clause in red in these sentences.

1. Last Sunday Denzil Ajay and Jackson who had forgotten his money started off for the swimming baths.

2. Opening his wallet Denzil gave Jackson some money.

3. The swimming pool in Palace Road was not far away.

4. When the teenagers arrived there was a queue.

- Now add commas where you think they should go in the sentences.

Remember

Commas separate:

- the main clause and the sub-clause
- extra words or phrases from the clause
- words in lists.

English Punctuation
© Folens (copiable page)

Activity sheet – Commas

Commas and clauses

☞ Add the sub-clause to these sentences.

Use the sign /\ to show you are inserting words.

Add commas where they are needed. For example:

> *who were locals,*
>
> Many people, /\ were at the swimming pool.
>
> **sub-clause:** 'who were locals'

1. The diving board was at the far end of the swimming pool.

   sub-clause: which was very high

2. Ajay jumped.

   sub-clause: who was not scared of heights

3. Denzil saw Ajay jump.

   sub-clause: who was watching

4. Ajay caused a huge splash

   sub-clause: which went everywhere.

5. Everybody nearby got splashed

   sub-clause: which meant there was a fuss.

6. The swimming attendant was not pleased.

   sub-clause: who was called Ray

'I have a pig with yellow wings'

I have a pig with yellow wings

I have a butterfly growing on my lawn

I have a weed of tartan cloth

I have a cloak laughing by the lake

I have a kookaburra leaping in the wind

I have a kite sailing down the stream

I have a leaf swinging from a string

I have a pearl as green as grass

I have a bullfrog beating on a drum

I have a toothache gentle as a breath

I have a melody without the tune

I have the words without the book

I have a tale within this poem

I have the answer to this riddle

Mary Green

(Based on 'I saw a peacock with a fiery tail', Anon., seventeenth century.)

English Punctuation

Teacher's notes

The apostrophe (1)

Objectives

- Understand why the apostrophe is used to shorten words
- Use the apostrophe appropriately to shorten words
- Use the shortened word 'it's' and the possessive 'its' correctly
- Learn what elision is

Prior knowledge

Students should be reading texts with expression. They should be writing in complex sentences and using a range of punctuation, including full stops, capital letters, question marks, exclamation marks and commas. Their handwriting should be legible.

English Framework links

Yr7 Sentence level 3, Writing 1; Yr8 Sentence level 3, Writing 1; Yr9 Sentence level 2

Scottish attainment targets

English Language – Writing
Strand – Knowledge about language
Level E

Background

The apostrophe is often wrongly used, either because it is wrongly placed or omitted altogether. When students are first introduced to it they often add it to an 's' regardless. Since most words that have the apostrophe can be understood without it, the apostrophe may well fall into disuse in the future. In this unit, however, the apostrophe to show omission is covered. This is easier for students to understand than the apostrophe to show possession, which is the focus of the next unit.

Starter activity

Find out how much students know about the apostrophe: whether they can name it and explain any of its functions. Present them with a sentence, for example: *I'll make the tea now, shall I?* Then ask students to identify all the punctuation in the sentence. Note how knowledgeable they are and where any misunderstandings occur.

Activity sheets

Use the activity sheet, 'Missing letters', to explain the function of the apostrophe to shorten words. Students can then identify all the shortened words in the conversation.

The second Activity sheet, 'Mix-up', deals with the confusion that often arises between 'it's' and the possessive 'its'.

The third Activity sheet, 'New words and old', looks at other ways the apostrophe is used to shorten words and also how the apostrophe can be dropped, as new words become incorporated into the language. You can follow this with the Activity sheet, 'More missing letters', which deals with elision. Students could keep a record of the common archaic words (many of which are covered on the Activity sheet) for use when reading Shakespeare texts. (Note that both 'e'en' and 'ev'n', meaning 'even', are listed.)

The last Activity sheet, 'Too many apostrophes', presents students with a film review that contains apostrophes used both correctly and incorrectly. Read the review with students first. They should spot and, where necessary, correct the mistakes. Answers are as follows: Correct: *O'Hara, he's, doesn't, there's, that's, 'Bout*; Incorrect: *live's, discover's, encourage's, thing's, lot's, Robb's, shot's*. Please note that this is a harder Activity sheet.

Plenary

Check students' understanding by giving them a series of words using the apostrophe. Choose those that haven't been used in the unit, for example: *she'll, d'you, isn't, we'd, wouldn't*.

Activity sheet – The apostrophe (1)

Missing letters

We often shorten words. When we do this in writing, we use the apostrophe. This tells us that letters have been left out. For example:

apostrophe   one letter, 'i', is dropped

that's   *that is*   *that is*

I'll   *I will*   *I will*

two letters, 'wi', are dropped

☞ Read the following. Underline in red all the words with the apostrophe. Write them out in full above.

FIRST FRIEND: <u>What's</u> the time?

SECOND FRIEND: It's 7:00pm.

FIRST FRIEND: They haven't rung then.

SECOND FRIEND: Stop worrying, they'll ring.

FIRST FRIEND: I bet they don't.

SECOND FRIEND: Why shouldn't they?
                    They said they'd ring.

FIRST FRIEND: Maybe they've forgotten.

SECOND FRIEND: They won't have forgotten.

FIRST FRIEND: Well, the phone hasn't rung, has it?

● Now read the conversation with the full words. Why do you think it sounds odd?

Activity sheet – The apostrophe (1)

Mix-up

People often mix up *it's* and *its*.

It's is a shortened word. Written fully, it reads: *it is* or *it has*. For example:

● *Where's the cat basket? It's not there.*

Its is one word and is used to show ownership. For example:

● *Give the cat its milk.*

☞ Read the following. Underline in red all the examples of *it's*.
Underline in blue all the examples of *its*.

AMY: It's hopeless. The cat won't come down from the tree. It's stuck and it's scared.

MARVIN: Where is it?

AMY: It's high up in the tree. Be careful of its claws!

MARVIN: I'll get the ladder. You get its cat basket.

(Marvin props the ladder against the tree and climbs up. The cat starts to spit.)

AMY: Don't hurt it, Marvin!

MARVIN: It's no good. I can't reach it.

(Cat lashes out with its paw.) Ouch!

(Cat leaps on Marvin. Ladder wobbles. Marvin falls. Cat lands safely.)

AMY: Poor puss! Poor puss! *(Cat purrs.)*

New words and old

Sometimes words that are shortened become new words. For example:

- *Halloween* was written as *Hallowe'en*. It meant *All Hallow Even* (evening).

Other words still use the apostrophe.
For example, a character in a story says:

- *"I'll meet you 'bout six."*

short for about

Some names and words also have an apostrophe.
For example:

- *O'Brien*   *O'* means 'of'

Remember
If we shorten words, we should show that letters are missing by using an apostrophe.

☞ Work with a partner to decide if these need an apostrophe or not. Check whether you are correct. Then add the apostrophes.

Macbeth	fraid not	Its his car.	mega-sized
O Donald	four o clock	DVD	Put the present in its box.
John O Groats	Frisby-on-the-Wreake	a cup o coffee	
O Connor	Ah, I see.	O Grady well-known BBC	

English Punctuation

Activity sheet – The apostrophe (1)

More missing letters

In poetry and plays from the past,
words were often shortened.
It helped to keep the rhythm of the line.
Where a letter was missing, an apostrophe
was used. For example:

- *oe'r* meaning 'over'

☞ Match the words on the left with their full versions on the right.
Look carefully! The first one has been done for you.

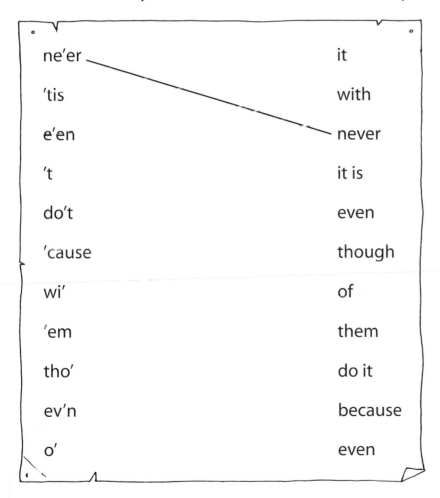

ne'er	it
'tis	with
e'en	never
't	it is
do't	even
'cause	though
wi'	of
'em	them
tho'	do it
ev'n	because
o'	even

- Write the full versions of these words. Do you know what they mean?

wither'd   Afric's   mellow'd   vex'd

_____   _____   _____   _____

Too many apostrophes

In the film review below, the apostrophe is used correctly but also incorrectly.

1. Find all the examples of the apostrophe.
2. Tick those that are correct.

    Use the proofreading sign *p* for those that are incorrect. Write the correct word underneath.

Drum Roll

120 mins
Cert 12A
Directed by: Justin Grey

Jay O'Hara, Kim Alex, Geena Scott, Nelson Robbs

Rufus (Jay O'Hara) live's in a one-horse town in the middle of nowhere. But he's got dreams and discover's, with help from his teacher Jack Marshall (Kim Alex), that he's talented too. Jack encourage's Rufus, a natural on the drums, to enter a music competition. He wins – but doesn't get the prize. Enter Claudia (Geena Scott). Then thing's start to hot up.

There's lot's going on in this movie, with a comic turn from Mikey played by Nelson Robb's, an up-and-coming young actor and one to watch. The camera work is also excellent. Its sweeping shot's of the mid-west landscape are breathtaking.

A wonderful movie, that's ideal for teenagers. 'Bout time too!

J.T.

Teacher's notes

The apostrophe (2)

Objectives

- Understand how the apostrophe is used to show ownership:
  - in the singular and plural
  - when the plural is not formed using 's'
  - for proper names and groups
- Use the apostrophe appropriately to show ownership

Prior knowledge

Students should be reading texts with expression. They should be writing in complex sentences and using a range of punctuation, including full stops, capital letters, question marks, exclamation marks and commas. Their handwriting should be legible.

English Framework links

Yr7 Sentence level 3, Writing 1; Yr8 Sentence level 3, Writing 1; Yr9 Sentence level 2

Scottish attainment targets

English Language – Writing
Strand – Knowledge about language
Level E

Background

Students usually find the apostrophe for ownership difficult to remember, even after they have grasped its purpose. The traditional memory prompt, 'The pen of my aunt/my aunt's pen', can still work for many students since it illustrates ownership. Using the apostrophe to show ownership in the plural presents an even greater conundrum for many students. For certain proper names (for example, ending in 's') and for groups, the apostrophe is often only remembered with practice.

Starter activity

If covered, recap on the main features of the apostrophe to shorten words (see the unit, 'The apostrophe (1)'). Then introduce the apostrophe for ownership by referring to the first activity sheet, 'Whose is it? (1)'. This deals with ownership in the singular only. Go through the explanation with students, not the tasks at this stage.

Resource sheet and Activity sheets

Following on from 'Starter activity', ask students to complete the Activity sheet, 'Whose is it? (1)' on their own. Check how well they've done. (The students could also keep the first half of the Resource sheet, 'Apostrophe tips', as a reference.)

Those who have coped well could go on to the next Activity sheet, 'Whose is it? (2)', but at a later date. It deals with the apostrophe for ownership in the plural and is more challenging. The second half of the Resource sheet, 'Apostrophe tips', may be useful here.

The Activity sheet, 'More plurals and apostrophes', is concerned with irregular plurals and how the apostrophe for possession is used with these. Please note other irregulars such as proper names (for example, Chris and Dave's house, Dickens' books) are not covered here.

The final Activity sheet, 'Going to the concert', is suitable for those students who have grasped the main features of using the apostrophe in different contexts.

Plenary

If the group you are working with is small, ask each student to think of two sentences in which the apostrophe for ownership is used. They should then write their sentences on the board, omitting the apostrophe, and ask others in the group to find the errors. They can refer to 'Apostrophe tips' for support. If you are teaching a larger group, select students for the task.

Whose is it? (1)

The apostrophe is used to show that a thing or things belong to someone or something else. For example:

<u>Sam's bike</u> was in the shed.   <u>Today's match</u> is off.

The bike belonging to Sam.   The match of today.

● Note where the apostrophe is.

☞ The following have apostrophes missing. Use the proofreading sign *p* to show where. Write the correct answer underneath.

The boys bag	Janes books	Rovers collar	
Last weeks newspaper	Leos job	Sues time	

☞ Correct these sentences in the same way. Write the correct answer underneath.

1. As it glided away, we could see the boats sail unfurl.

_____

2. The rivers source was somewhere in the mountains.

_____

3. Most of the Earths surface is covered in water.

_____

4. A rivers channel carries great volumes of water.

_____

5. Todays sunshine means Devons beaches will be crammed.

_____

English Punctuation

Whose is it? (2)

Remember

The apostrophe is used to show that a thing or things belong to someone or something else. For example:

Sam's bike was in the shed.   Today's match is off.

   The bike belonging to Sam.   The match of today.

- Note where the apostrophe is.

If a thing or things belong to **more than one** person or thing the apostrophe changes places.

The boys' bikes were in the shed.

      The bikes belong to the boys.

- Note where the apostrophe has shifted.

---

1. Read the passage below. The apostrophes to show ownership by **more than one** person or thing are missing.

2. Use the proofreading sign *p* to show where the apostrophes should go.

3. Write the changes underneath.

Polly was going to visit her two aunts in a nearby village. Her aunts bungalow

was at the end of Elm Road. When she arrived she couldn't believe what she saw. The

road was full of police and reporters. Car-windows had been smashed

and there was glass everywhere. Neighbours dustbins were all over the road.

Witnesses statements were being taken and residents comments were being

recorded. It had all happened during the night and no one knew how or why.

Apostrophe tips

> **Remember**
> A singular is one thing (*boy*).
> A plural is more than one thing (*boys*).

The <u>boy</u> ran down the street.

This is a singular, not a plural.

It doesn't show belonging. It has no apostrophe.

The <u>boy's</u> dog ran with him.

This is a singular, not a plural.

It does show belonging. The dog belongs to the boy.

So it has an apostrophe.

●   Every time you use the apostrophe ask yourself: Do I need to show belonging?

Apostrophe tips

We often confuse when to use the apostrophe with plurals.

> **Remember**
> A singular is one thing (*boy*).
> A plural is more than one thing (*boys*).

We don't use the apostrophe with every plural.

The <u>boys</u> ran down the street.

This is a plural. It doesn't show belonging.

It has no apostrophe.

The <u>boys'</u> dogs ran with them.

This is a plural. It does show belonging.

The dogs belong to the boys.

So it has an apostrophe.

●   Every time you use the apostrophe ask yourself: Do I need to show belonging?

English Punctuation

More plurals and apostrophes

> **Remember**
> Singular = one   Plural = more than one

We don't always form the plural by adding 's'. For example:

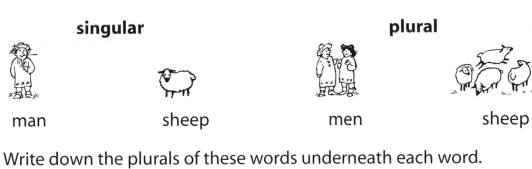

singular		**plural**	
man	sheep	men	sheep

☞ Write down the plurals of these words underneath each word.

mouse	foot	deer	tooth	goose	woman	child

To show the apostrophe for ownership with these plurals we add 's' to them. For example:

● *Men's clothes are on the third floor of the shop.*

☞ Use the plurals you made above to show the apostrophe for ownership. Write sentences with them in.

1. _____

2. _____

3. _____

4. _____

5. _____

6. _____

7. _____

Going to the concert

Write a conversation between two friends.

Give them names.

Here's an example:

(Name of First Friend): Are you still going to the concert tonight?

Apostrophe to shorten words

(Name of Second Friend): Yeah! I <u>wouldn't</u> miss it for anything.

Have you heard _Lenny Cool's_ new album?

Apostrophe for ownership

Include some of these in your conversation:

Apostrophe to shorten words

| couldn't | o'clock | it's | isn't | won't | d'you | they'll | we'll |

Apostrophe for ownership

| the band's | the club's | parents' | people's |

Conversation

_____

_____

_____

_____

_____

_____

_____

_____

_____

Teacher's notes

Direct speech

Objectives

- Understand that direct speech refers to the actual words spoken
- Understand the function of speech marks
- Learn where to include other punctuation when using speech marks
- Learn to vary vocabulary
- Learn that a new paragraph is used when another voice speaks

Prior knowledge

Students should be able to recognise sentences, read simple texts with expression and write in sentences using full stops, capital letters, question marks and exclamation marks. Their handwriting should be legible.

English Framework links

Yr7 Sentence level 3, 8; Yr8 Sentence level 3, 6; Yr9 Sentence level 2, 4, 6

Scottish attainment targets

English Language – Writing
Strand – Punctuation and structure
Level D

Background

Students (of all abilities) often find it tricky to punctuate direct speech correctly in writing. Sometimes this is because they have not grasped the function of the speech marks and assume that all words are contained within them, including the reported element, for example: "Where are you going? she said." The habit can persist. One of the best ways to overcome this is to begin teaching speech marks by using speech bubbles. The bubble seems to act as an effective barrier, separating direct speech and the reported words.

Starter activity

Bring in some teenage magazines or comics that have cartoons and speech bubbles. Point out that the words in the speech bubbles are the words actually spoken. This will reinforce the work in the first few Activity sheets for those students who have not grasped what direct speech is. For those who have some skills in using speech marks, ask them to show how we would present 'cartoon speech' in continuous writing.

Activity sheets

The first two Activity sheets, 'What are they saying? (1)' and '(2)', should be used together. They are aimed at those students who have little or no idea how to use speech marks. Others with more advanced skills will not need to complete them.

The Activity sheet, 'Speech marks and other punctuation', shows students what punctuation is included within speech marks, while the Activity sheet, 'Said, said, said', encourages students to use a range of vocabulary to show who has spoken. Adverbs as well as verbs are included, although some students may wish to choose their own.

In the final Activity sheet, 'A new line', students must extend a conversation using what they have learned and remembering to begin a new line when a new person speaks. This is considerably more difficult than earlier Activity sheets.

Plenary

Recap on the essential features of direct speech in continuous writing, according to the skills students have covered.

What are they saying? (1)

1. Read what Gina and her mum are saying. Then complete the speech bubbles.

2. Write your own speech bubbles. Then add who said the words outside the bubbles.

English Punctuation

Activity sheet – Direct speech

What are they saying? (2)

We use **speech marks** to show the words people are saying.

"What on earth do you think you're doing?" said Gina's mum.

Speech marks are like speech bubbles. They contain the words spoken.

These words are outside the speech marks. They are not the words spoken. They tell us who said the words.

☞ Finish the rest of the conversation from the Activity sheet, 'What are they saying? (1)'. Use speech marks. Add who said the words.

Nothing _____

Nothing! Is that my purse? _____

Don't be angry, Mum, please _____

_____

_____

_____

_____

_____

_____

_____

_____

_____

Speech marks and other punctuation

What happens to other punctuation when we use speech marks?
Where should it be put?

"Nothing! Is that my purse?" said Gina's mum.

Exclamation marks, **question marks** and
also **full stops** go inside the speech marks.

● Where a **comma** goes can change.

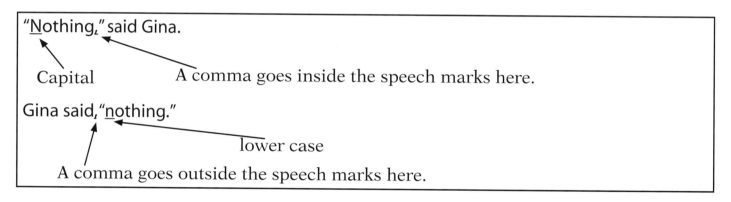

"Nothing," said Gina.

Capital   A comma goes inside the speech marks here.

Gina said, "nothing."

lower case

A comma goes outside the speech marks here.

☞ Put the speech marks and all the missing punctuation in the correct places in the
sentences.

1.   I'll meet you at the cinema said Yusef

2.   Chris said we'll have to hurry up if we're going to get there in time

3.   Oh no Are we going to be late shouted Kelly

4.   We should make it if we leave now Chris said looking at his watch

5.   Where have you been called Yusef when he saw his two friends

6.   It's a good thing I bought the tickets he added

English Punctuation

Said, said, said

We do not always have to use 'said'.
We can vary our words.

"Did you guess what had happened?" he **asked**.
"I have to admit, it wasn't a surprise," she **replied**.

or

"Did you guess what had happened?" he **asked, raising his eyebrows**.
"I have to admit, it wasn't a surprise," she **replied, knowingly**.

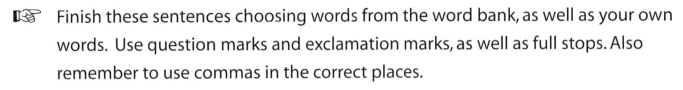 Finish these sentences choosing words from the word bank, as well as your own words. Use question marks and exclamation marks, as well as full stops. Also remember to use commas in the correct places.

1. "Well, what's

    _____

2. "I don't

    _____

3. "Simone

    _____

4. "I haven't

    _____

5. He

    _____

6. "Certainly

    _____

7. She

    _____

Word bank						
asked	replied	called	laughed	sighed	groaned	continued
uncomfortably	despairingly	loudly	carefully	happily	sadly	confidently

A new line

When a new person speaks we start a new line.

Cal dashed down the road from school. He had to get home before his older brother, Jerry. When he got to the end of Bell Lane he turned the corner at top speed and crashed straight into – Jerry.

"Watch out idiot!" shouted Jerry, grabbing Cal by his sweater, "Look where you're going." Jerry was tall and mean, not somebody you would choose to bump into.

"Sorry," muttered Cal. He was squirming under Jerry's grip. "Let me go!"

"Give me one good reason why," sneered Jerry.

new lines

☞ Carry on the conversation between Cal and Jerry. Begin:

"I … I have to get home," pleaded Cal. He didn't want to say why, of course.

Teacher's notes

Indirect speech

Objectives

- Understand that indirect speech is speech that is reported
- Convert direct speech into indirect speech
- Learn that indirect speech may not contain the actual words spoken, but should contain the meaning

Prior knowledge

Students should be reading texts with expression and be writing in sentences using full stops, capital letters, question marks and exclamation marks. Their handwriting should be legible.

English Framework links

Yr7 Sentence level 1; Yr8 Sentence level 1; Yr9 Sentence level 4

Scottish attainment targets

English Language – Writing
Strand – Punctuation and structure
Level D
Strand – Knowledge about language
Level E
Strand – Functional writing
Level D

Background

Writing in indirect speech can prove tricky if students are unaware of how to use clauses correctly. The 'that clause' is frequently used in declaratives. For example: *He said that trying to cover up the truth would, in the circumstances, be foolish.* However, 'that' is often omitted after many verbs. *He told her I jumped over the wall and ran away.* In interrogatives 'that' may be replaced by 'what' and other 'wh' words. *He asked what/ why etc.* There are many ways of expressing speech indirectly. However, if students at this stage keep 'that' in their minds when trying to write in indirect speech, it will act as a rough guide.

Starter activity

Ask students to describe some of the features of direct speech if they have completed the unit, 'Direct speech'. Then discuss the difference between direct and indirect speech by explaining the terms. Refer to the definition on the first Activity sheet 'He said that…' and complete the three questions with students.

Resource sheet and Activity sheets

The second Activity sheet, 'Turn around', and the third, "Knock, knock, who's there?", contain both direct and indirect speech. You can note if and where students experience difficulties.

The fourth Activity sheet, 'Writing a report', involves only indirect speech but is more challenging. Read the first paragraph with students and discuss what residents are likely to say. Students can make notes and complete the frame. Also remind students not to use direct speech, for example in the case of 'the owner of The Flag pub said'. Here they would need to add 'that'.

The Resource sheet, 'Presenting speech in different ways' contains a passage from a playscript, which is also rewritten as prose in direct and indirect speech. You can contrast all three examples or select only two for contrast. Go through the annotations and ask students to find other examples in each text. Students can keep the sheet as a resource. See also Plenary below.

Plenary

Remind students that direct speech cannot always be 'translated' to good effect, for example when telling a joke. The text in the Activity sheet, "Knock, knock, who's there?" includes an example of this. Give students an indirect version of this and encourage students to see that the joke has been lost. For example: *There was a knock at the door. Kenny asked who was there and Yasmin replied that it was Carrie …*

Activity sheet – Indirect speech

He said that …

Indirect speech is a report of what has been said. It is sometimes called reported speech. Compare the direct and indirect speech below.

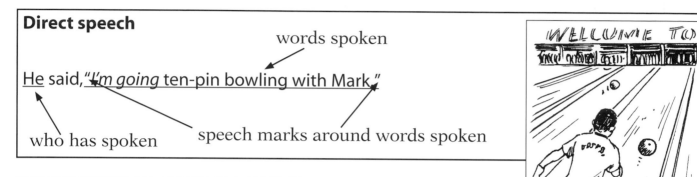

Direct speech

words spoken

He said, "*I'm going* ten-pin bowling with Mark."

who has spoken

speech marks around words spoken

Indirect speech

'that' helps us to report what has been said

He said <u>that</u> *he was going* ten-pin bowling with Mark.

- The speech marks have gone.
- *I'm going* (first-person pronoun and present tense verb) has become *he was going* (third-person pronoun and past tense verb).

Indirect speech does not have to contain the actual words spoken. However, it should still have the same meaning. For example:

Direct speech	Indirect speech
He said, "yes."	He agreed.

☞ How would you change these sentences from direct to indirect speech? Work in a group to decide.

1. Jane said, "We're going on holiday tomorrow."

   _____

   _____

2. "Definitely not," said Mum, "you can't go."

   _____

   _____

3. "Oh! Thank goodness you're back!" said Dad.

   _____

   _____

Activity sheet – Indirect speech

Turn around

☞ The following are written in indirect speech.
Rewrite them in direct speech underneath.

1. She asked her brother if she could use his mobile.

   _____

   _____

2. Dad said he would take us out for a meal on Saturday.

   _____

   _____

3. Kayla said that they found the dog in Wood Road.

   _____

   _____

4. He agreed to play in the match on Friday.

   _____

   _____

☞ The following is written in direct speech. Rewrite it in indirect speech in the box.

"I've finished my project, Miss," called out Marlon.

"Well, you'd better read it out to the whole class," said Miss Smart.

So Marlon stood up and announced, "I'm going to treat you all to
'The History of the Carp'."

"What's a carp?" asked Joline, pulling a face.

"You're about to find out," replied Marlon confidently.

Activity sheet – Indirect speech

"Knock knock, who's there?"

☞ Read the conversation below.

Yasmin looked straight at Kenny. She said that Jake was a real comic. She put the stress on real. She said that although his jokes were daft, she, for one, thought they were funny, adding that it was all to do with the way he told them.

Kenny stared back astonished. Jake? What was Yasmin talking about? Jake had no sense of humour at all.

"What?" Kenny muttered.

"Listen to this one, then," said Yasmin, "Knock, knock!"

Kenny said nothing.

"Go on," said Yasmin.

"Who's there?" muttered Kenny half-heartedly.

"Carrie."

"Carrie who?" said Kenny in a weary voice.

But before Yasmin could deliver the punchline, there was a tap on her shoulder. Yasmin and Kenny swung round to see a beaming smile. It was none other than the joker himself.

1. Find examples of direct speech and underline in blue:

   ● the words spoken   ● who has spoken them.

2. Put a ring round:

   ● an example of speech marks
   ● other examples of punctuation inside the speech marks.

3. Find examples of indirect speech. Underline in red an example of:

   ● 'that'   ● the third person   ● the past tense

English Punctuation

Activity sheet – Indirect speech

Writing a report

You are a TV reporter at the scene of some floods.
You have interviewed several people,
so you are reporting what they have told you.
Use this writing frame to write your report
in indirect speech.

The crew and I arrived at 10:00am at the small town of St Ann's-in-the-Vale, where the River Vee has broken its banks. The high street is completely waterlogged. Most people have been moved out.

Several local residents told us that _____

_____

One resident, who has lived here all his life, commented _____

_____

A local farmer, Jack Dodds, _____

_____

and the owner of 'The Flag' pub said _____

_____

We also interviewed Bert Cole from the environment agency who _____

_____

and agreed that _____

_____

No more rain is forecast at present and the water is beginning to subside.

Presenting speech in different ways

Below are examples of the same conversation written in different ways.

Script   who is speaking   Words spoken, no speech marks

DAVID: *(crossly)* Look, I'm an easy-going person, Kisha. But you're beginning to get on my nerves – big time.

KISHA: I didn't ask you to do this! I didn't ask you to take me out – like I was six or something and couldn't look after myself. Did I?

stage directions

from *She's No Saint* by Mary Green

Direct speech   speech marks around words spoken

"I'm an easy-going person, but you're beginning to get on my nerves – big time," said David to Kisha.

"I didn't ask you to do this!" retorted Kisha. "I didn't ask you to take me out – like I was six or something and couldn't look after myself. Did I?"

who has spoken

new line when someone new speaks   example of words spoken

Indirect speech   beginning of 'that' clause

David said to Kisha that he was an easy-going person, but that she was beginning to get on his nerves – big time. Kisha retorted that she hadn't asked him to take her out, as though she was six years old and couldn't look after herself.

more formal language than speech   has changed to third-person past tense

English Punctuation   © Folens (copiable page)

Teacher's notes

Miscellaneous punctuation

Objectives

- Learn the functions of the following selected punctuation: colon, semicolon, hyphen, dash, brackets

Prior knowledge

Students should be reading texts with expression and be writing in sentences using full stops, capital letters, question marks and exclamation marks. They should also be aware of a range of other punctuation (such as the apostrophe and direct speech) and be attempting to use it. Their handwriting should be legible.

English Framework links

Yr7 Sentence level 3, Writing 1; Yr8 Sentence level 3, Writing 1; Yr9 Sentence level 2

Scottish attainment targets

English Language – Writing
Strand – Punctuation and structure
Level D

Background

This unit covers punctuation that tends to occur in complex sentences and more sophisticated writing. It is suitable for students who have made good progress and are working towards extending their range. However, there are some contexts that most students will find accessible, for example the use of the colon to introduce a list, or its use in scripts to signal the speaker, as well as the use of the hyphen to create compound words. (A compound word can become a single word, a hyphenated word or two separate words that act as a compound, such as *cleaning fluid*.) You will need to decide which Activity sheets are suitable for which students.

Starter activity

Introduce the colon by referring to the first Activity sheet, 'The colon'. Explain the colon's two main functions.

Activity sheets

On the first Activity sheet, 'The colon', Students should have no difficulty in recognising the colon. They could continue the script in pairs, taking a role each. Using the semicolon is more difficult and is presented on the Activity sheet, 'The semicolon', for those students sufficiently confident to tackle it. They should be able to match the sentences, but they may have greater difficulty writing their own. Remind them to drop the capital letter in the second sentence, except where sentences begin with names.

On the Activity sheet, 'The hyphen', note whether the students are unfamiliar with any of the words and whether they can distinguish between the compound words and the descriptions.

The fourth Activity sheet is 'The dash'. Students may find the dash difficult to separate from the comma, as their functions are very similar. The former has a sharper pause. As students write their notes they will need to create a sense of speed. Point to the double meaning of 'dash' as a useful prompt.

The final Activity sheet, 'Brackets', explains the use of this form of punctuation. Point out to students that the information enclosed is not necessary to the sentence; it will make sense without it. Encourage students to realise that if brackets are not included, ambiguity can result.

Plenary

Provide students with some playscripts to look through. Ask them to identify the colon and explain its use. Recap on any other punctuation covered, asking students to give examples.

The colon

This is a colon : It is a pause.

Sometimes it is used to list information. For example:

> *Collect together all the equipment: pens, pencils, rulers, rubbers and paintbrushes.*
>
> colon

 The colon is missing from **two** of these sentences. Use the proofreading sign *p* to show where it should go. Then add the colon.

1. I want you to use a world map to find these countries China, India, Russia, the USA and Australia.

2. To fix the problem you will need some tools a hammer, a drill, a pair of pliers and some scissors.

3. Three pairs of socks, a pair of trainers, a sweater and two CDs were packed in his case.

 A colon is also used in scripts.

Interviewer: Well now, Miss … er … Miss …
(*looking at some papers*)

Interviewee: Miss Lott.

Interviewer: Ah yes, yes. Here we have it.
(*opening a file*) Miss … er … Miss
Blot.

Interviewee: Lott. The name is Lott.

Interviewer: Indeed … yes … Thank you … er … Miss Rot …

- Finish the script on another sheet of paper. Write about ten more lines. Use the colon.

- Also include the colon to list information in the script. Create the list yourself.

English Punctuation

The semicolon

This is a semicolon **;**

It is used within a sentence. For example:

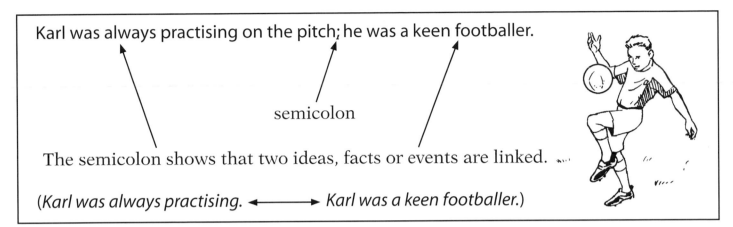

Karl was always practising on the pitch; he was a keen footballer.

semicolon

The semicolon shows that two ideas, facts or events are linked.

(*Karl was always practising.* ←—→ *Karl was a keen footballer.*)

1. Match each sentence in column 1 with its correct partner in column 2.

Column 1	Column 2
She was going to be very late.	He buys cheap shoes.
On the one hand she had money.	He liked to stay at home.
He buys stylish suits.	Being late was a regular habit.
Sam had three brothers.	On the other she didn't want to spend it.
She loved adventure.	Tom had five.

2. On another sheet of paper, write out the sentences using a semicolon.

3. Write two sentences of your own using the semicolon.

The hyphen

This is a hyphen -

It is used to join words (or sometimes letters and words).

This often happens when we use certain words together a lot.
In this way they become compound words.
For example: *twenty-six*

Some of the words below need hyphens.
Others are only adjectives describing nouns.
For example: *sunny day*

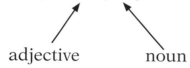

adjective   noun

☞ Sort the words into two groups below headed:
'Hyphens'/'Adjectives and nouns'.

Add hyphens to those that need it.

passer by	sleeping dog	fancy food	thirty six	X ray
anti war	half truth	T shirt	large hat	tall men
ninety five	silky dress	one month old	red jacket	CD cover

Hyphens	Adjectives and nouns

English Punctuation

© Folens (copiable page)

Activity sheet – Miscellaneous punctuation

The dash

The dash can be used to create a pause in a sentence, like a comma.

But its pause is more sudden. Work out what the following means:

Red Jackdaw – five to one – fifty quid – lost the lot!

☞ Read the notes and cards on the noticeboard below. They all need dashes. Use the proofreading sign *p* to show where. Then add the dashes.

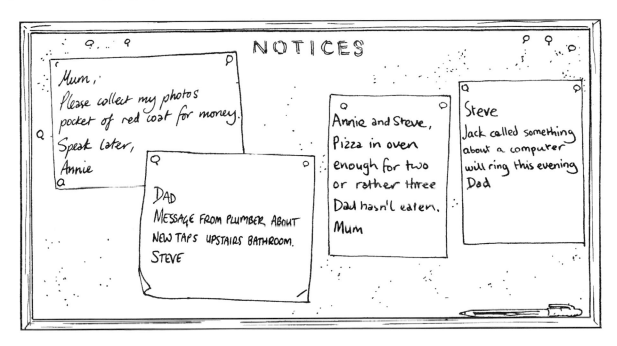

☞ Now write replies to each of the notes on this noticeboard. Use dashes.

Activity sheet – Miscellaneous punctuation

Brackets

These are brackets ( )

Brackets enclose information that is set apart from the rest of the sentence. Without brackets, the meaning of the sentence may be unclear. For example:

- *Madrid is the capital of Spain (see map) and Paris is the capital of France.*

☞ Put brackets in the right places in the sentences. Use a red pen.

1. We left at 6:00am I was hardly awake and arrived at midnight so we were all very tired.

2. Steve is in a bad mood with Molly nothing new there because she borrowed his camera without asking.

3. The photos Steve's works of art are all of the beach and sea front.

☞ The brackets are in the wrong places in these sentences. Use the proofreading sign *p* to show the mistakes. Then add the brackets in the correct places using a red pen.

1. Dad's new bike old one has gone to the dump (is a racing bike) with more gears than he can use.

2. Gran has a motorbike it goes like the wind that she travels to work on (three days a week).

3. Yesterday Harry announced you wouldn't believe it (that he was going skiing) whatever the cost.

☞ On another sheet of paper, write sentences with the following in them.

1. (see diagram below)

2. (he won second prize last year)

3. (his sister is Steve's friend)

4. (photo over page)

Teacher's notes

Odds and ends

Objectives

- Understand the need for punctuation to make sense of what is read
- Use punctuation (or its absence) creatively
- Revise: capital letters, full stops, commas, question marks, exclamation marks, the apostrophe (both uses), direct speech and indirect speech

Prior knowledge

Students should be reading texts with expression and be writing in sentences using full stops, capital letters, question marks and exclamation marks. They should also be aware of a range of other punctuation (such as the apostrophe and direct speech) and be attempting to use it. Their handwriting should be legible.

English Framework links

Yr7 Sentence level 3, Writing 1; Yr8 Sentence level 3, Writing 1; Yr9 Sentence level 2

Scottish attainment targets

English Language – Writing
Strand – Knowledge about language
Level D
Strand – Punctuation and structure
Level D
Strand – Functional writing
Level C

Background

This unit is a revision unit covering a range of punctuation (see Objectives). It also reminds students of the need for accurate punctuation, while presenting them with ways in which punctuation (or the lack of it) can be used creatively.

Starter activity

Quickly recap students' knowledge of the punctuation covered throughout the units. For example, ask them: *What do all sentences start with? What finishes a sentence? (Think of more than one way.) When do we use apostrophes? What words are included within speech marks? What is a colon? When do we use it? Think of an example*, and so on.

Resource sheet and Activity sheets

The first Activity sheet, 'Check it!', is easier than the following, 'Check it again'. These revision sheets should be used according to the students' individual abilities. As far as possible, the students should complete the exercises on their own. This should provide an idea of a student's strengths and weaknesses.

Illustrate the need for punctuation by referring to John Foster's puzzle poem on the Resource sheet, 'whatspunctuation'. First begin by asking students what punctuation the title should have (*What's Punctuation?*). Depending upon the students' abilities, they could work out the meaning on their own, with a partner, or as a group with the aid of an adult. (The following are missing: capital letters, full stops, apostrophes, question mark, comma. The exclamation mark or a comma could be included after 'yes'.)

In the final Activity sheet, 'Problem postcard', students can create their own non-punctuation postcard, using John Foster's poem as a model. They should write it correctly first and then redraft it without punctuation, ideally using ICT.

Plenary

Ask students to read their postcards aloud. If students are working in a small group, it would be useful if they all had a print-out of each postcard to follow as it is being read. When finished, discuss the usefulness of punctuation.

Check it!

Proofreading signs

What can you remember?

☰	capital letter	⊙	full stop
p	punctuation mistake	//	new paragraph

Full stops and capital letters

Use proofreading signs to show where capital letters, full stops, commas and a new paragraph should go.

a lion was seen in batby high street today shocked passers-by took cover traffic ground to a halt the lion an elderly beast strode along without so much as a glance at frightened shoppers the owner sir godfrey tootle coaxed the animal into his lorry and they returned to his wildlife park at tootle hall

Question marks and exclamation marks

The following need a question mark or an exclamation mark.
Add the correct ones.

Hi   Where have you been   It'll be all right, won't it

The snow came tumbling down. Crash   Did she collect the tickets

Apostrophes

Correct the words. Then write the full version.

	correction	full version
wouldnt		
Im		
wont		
doesnt		
hes		

English Punctuation

Activity sheet – Odds and ends

Check it again

Proofreading signs

What can you remember?

☰	capital letter	⊙	full stop	
p	punctuation mistake	/	new line	// new paragraph

Apostrophes

Correct the words by adding an apostrophe in the right place.

<table>
<tr><td></td><td>**correction**</td></tr>
<tr><td>The childrens bags were lost.</td><td>_____</td></tr>
<tr><td>It was Ashoks brother who won.</td><td>_____</td></tr>
<tr><td>Last weeks news is out of date.</td><td>_____</td></tr>
<tr><td>Shes taken Megans pen.</td><td>_____</td></tr>
<tr><td>All the books covers were torn.</td><td>_____</td></tr>
</table>

Direct speech

Use the proofreading signs to find the mistakes.

Then write out the passage correctly on a separate sheet of paper.

> Quickly pass the key to me Jamie said. What are you going to do? asked Mia
>
> Well first see if the key fits and if it does go inside he replied. Do you think that's wise?
>
> Mia asked frowning. What else do you suggest? he retorted.

Indirect speech

Change the following direct speech to indirect speech.

- "I'll be coming to visit you soon," said Demos.

  _____

- Sita said, "It'll take me thirty minutes to get there."

  _____

- "How many cheese rolls should I make?" asked Luke.

  _____

'whatspunctuation'

whatspunctuationweallneed

itsothatwecanread

whatotherswritewithoutitwed

besoconfusedwewouldnotknow

ifweshouldstoporgo

onreadingwewouldlosetheflow

ofwhatthewritermeanttosay

yeswedallloseourway

sopunctuationsheretostay

John Foster

English Punctuation

Problem postcard

1. Write a message for a postcard with the address of the person you would send it to.
    (Make up an address if you prefer.)
    Write your postcard on separate paper first.
    Include the following:

    - capital letters and full stops
    - a question mark
    - an exclamation mark
    - apostrophes to shorten words.

2. When you have written your postcard, write it out, *without the punctuation*, using ICT.
    Use the Resource sheet, 'whatspunctuation' as a model.
    Also create a postcard layout using ICT. Use the one below to help you.

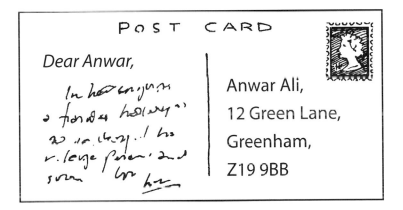

3. Ask a partner to work out what your postcard says.
    He or she should read it to you.

4. Check your partner's reading against your punctuated message.

Word bank

| hotel | coast | village | town | water | sports | sailing |
| swimming | beach ball | shark | jellyfish | seaweed | rock pool | shells |

Assessment sheet

Tick the boxes to show what you know or can do.

	know/ yes	not sure/ sometimes	don't know/ no
1. I listen to the teacher.			
2. I can work well with a partner.			
3. I can work well in a group.			
4.			
5.			
6.			
7.			
8.			
9.			
10.			

I know best/I can do best:

....

....

I need to: **(Write no more than three targets.)**

....

....

....